For my mother, Ernestine Lenora Cline  —L.C-R.

For my sweet potato, Malcolm Grant  —J.E.R.

LESA CLINE-RANSOME

# SATCHEL PAIGE

paintings by JAMES E. RANSOME

ALADDIN PAPERBACKS
New York London Toronto Sydney Singapore

**S**ome say Leroy Paige was born six feet three and a half inches tall, 180 pounds, wearing a size fourteen shoe. Not a bit of truth to it. And some argue that when Mrs. Lula Paige first held her precious Leroy in her arms, she noticed his right fist was tightly curled around a baseball. Pure fiction. It would take him eighteen years to grow to that size and about half that amount of time to realize that his hand and a baseball were a perfect match.

He knew from early on he had a gift for throwing. His mom, Lula, knew it, too. When she needed a plump chicken for the evening's supper, she'd send her Leroy to do the fetching. His arm, so strong and lean, was as swift and sure as any rifle. With a rock he could knock a chicken or most anything else out with one shot.

By the time Leroy was ten he could outthrow anyone, small or grown. He spent all his free time practicing, and it showed. He pitched a shutout game the first time he stepped onto the mound as pitcher for the W. H. Council School team in Mobile, Alabama. Folks would talk about that Paige boy over on the South Side long after a game had ended.

Even with baseball keeping him as busy as it did, earning money was always on young Leroy's mind. As the seventh of twelve Paige children, he understood he had to do his part to put food on the table. Leroy knew that the pennies earned from his bottle collecting wouldn't be enough to help support his family, so he headed out to the depot, where he'd heard some real money could be made.

At the depot, Leroy's pennies soon turned into shiny new dimes tossed from the hands of passengers returning to Mobile from faraway places like Chicago, Baltimore, and New Orleans. He was always the first and fastest to offer his toting services. And when he began to hang a half dozen or so satchels on a long stick that he draped over his shoulders, his friends told him he looked just like a walking satchel tree. Somehow, the name "Satchel" just stuck.

When dimes weren't enough, Leroy took to stealing. And when he could no longer run fast enough, it was stealing that caught him. Shortly after Leroy's twelfth birthday he was sent off to a place far beyond rural roads and depot dimes.

Life at the Mount Meigs Industrial School for Negro Children was difficult for most, but not for Satchel. He was surprised at how good a hard, honest day's work could make him feel. And the best thing about reform school (aside from the three meals a day and a pair of shoes) was the baseball team.

He'd certainly played his share of games with his buddies back on the streets of Mobile, but, you see, they were nothing like this. Real leather balls (not the ones your mama made with a rock and a rag) and real wooden bats, too. After seeing him try out for the school team, the coach at Mount Meigs kept his eye on young Satchel and taught him the difference between throwing and pitching. "You concentrate on baseball," he told Satchel, "and you might make something of yourself."

Satchel kept right on pitching up until 1923, the year he returned to his family's little house on Bascombe Street. He'd been gone six years, but he still knew what it meant when his mom told him, "We got mouths to feed." There weren't many career choices for blacks in the segregated South, and not one of those choices appealed to Satch. Besides, baseball was all he knew.

He made his way over to the stadium where his big brother, Wilson "Paddlefoot" Paige, was playing for the black semipro team the Mobile Tigers, and he talked the coach into letting him try out. Ten pitches and ten strikes later, he was their new starting pitcher. The pay was small, and the crowds even smaller, but it was baseball, plain and simple.

After just a few games Satch became so sure of his pitching he'd bet anyone who'd listen he could knock ten bottles off a wall or throw ten straight pitches over a hankie. The extra money he made from winning bets wasn't much, but it was more than a dime a satchel, and more than he'd ever had before.

As a semipro pitcher, Satchel developed his own unique style. He'd pick up a tip here and there, put his Satchel spin on it, and polish it off with a brand-new name. Got so Satch began to think of his pitches as his children. The "hesitation" was his magic slow ball. The "trouble ball" caused all sorts of havoc. And then there was the "bee ball," which, according to Satch, would "always be where I want it to be."

There was an odd way about his pitching. He would stand tall and straight as an oak tree on the mound. His foot looked to be about a mile long, and when he shot it into the air, it seemed to block out the sun. Satch's arm seemed to stretch on forever, winding, bending, twisting. And then there was that grin he flashed just as he released the ball. It seemed to say, "Go ahead, just try and get a hit off of that."

"Strike one!"

And you never saw it coming. I mean, one minute it was there, plain as day in his hand, and then, all of a sudden . . .

"Strike two!"

It was in the catcher's mitt. The batter would strain his eyes, squint a little.

Here it comes, got it now.

"Strike three!"

Just like that. All over.

"Next batter up!"

"Give it to 'em, Satch. Show your stuff," fans and teammates
would shout. And he did. Every time. Folks would pack the stands to
see how many Satchel could strike out in one game. He made the
crowds laugh with his fast talking and slow walking ("A man's got to
go slow to go long and far," he'd say), but mostly he made them
cheer. Never in his nineteen years had he heard a sweeter sound.
The more cheers he heard, the more his confidence grew. A kind of

confidence that made him call to the outfield with the bases loaded
and the last hitter up to bat, "Why don't you all have a seat. Won't
be needing you on this one."

Wherever the crowds went, a good paycheck followed, so he
made sure to keep them coming. After just one year he was playing
in the Negro major leagues for the Chattanooga Black Lookouts, and
the folks were still cheering and shouting, "Give it to 'em, Satch.
Show your stuff."

There were two major leagues back in 1924, when Satchel was called up. Because the white major-league ball clubs wouldn't allow blacks to play in their leagues, blacks had created their own in 1920 and named them the Negro Leagues. The white major-league players enjoyed trains, hotels, hot meals, and short seasons.

Negro League players were often refused meals in restaurants and rooms in hotels. They ate on the road and slept where they could—in train depots or on baseball fields. They played two, sometimes three games a day, nearly every day, in a season as long as the weather would hold. And when the season ended in America, Satch went right on playing and traveling in other parts of the world.

Life in the Negro Leagues suited Satchel. He was a traveling man. One city could never hold him for long. He moved from Alabama, where he played with the Birmingham Black Barons, to Tennessee, where he played with the Nashville Elite Giants, and to Pennsylvania, where he played with the Pittsburgh Crawfords.

From the first breath of spring till the cool rush of fall he would ride. Sometimes he joined his teammates on rickety old buses, bumping along on back roads studded with potholes so deep, players would have to hold on to their seats (and stomachs) just to keep from spilling into the aisles. But mostly he drove alone, in cars that would take him wherever he wanted to go. The fans would always be waiting in the next town. Their wait could be a long one— he was never much for keeping anyone's time but his own.

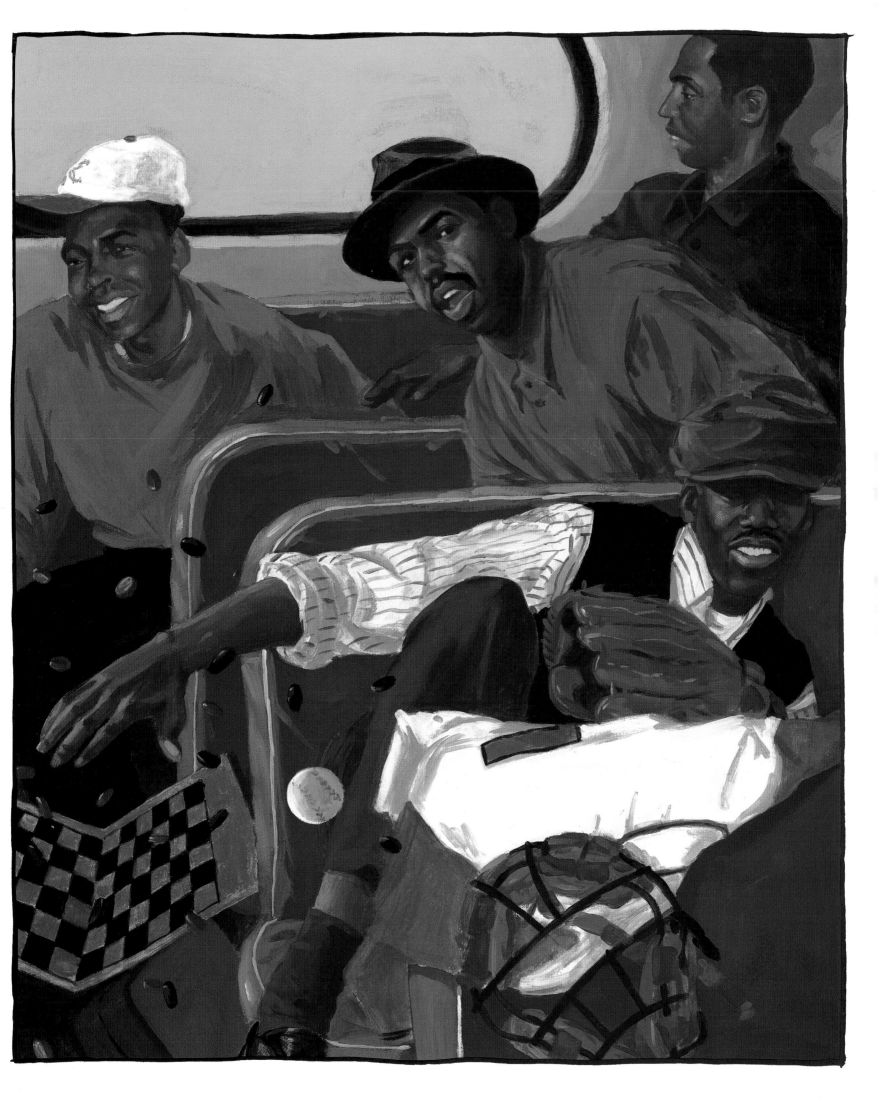

Once he reached his mid-thirties, the joys of traveling began to wear thin for Satchel. He found himself longing for a more settled life and the comforts of a home. In 1941 he finally found it in the warm smile and tender heart of Lahoma Brown. Satch rested his travel-weary legs and happily began his second career as husband and father. But even though he had finally found what he thought he'd been searching for, it was only a year before he took to the road again with his first and only true love—baseball. His family would have to wait.

Satchel's teammates were in love with the game, too. And out of
that love grew players better than anyone could ever dream. His
teammates included "Cool Papa" Bell, a hitter who ran bases so fast, if
you blinked you'd swear he'd never left home plate. Oscar Charleston
was an outfielder who could tell just where a ball would land as soon
as it hit the bat. And then there was Josh Gibson, who some said
could hit a ball so hard and so far, it would land somewhere in the
middle of next week. Because of his powerful hitting and home run
record, Josh was sometimes called "the black Babe Ruth," but many

wondered if the Babe should have been called "the white Josh Gibson."

Back in 1923, when Gibson and Satch were teammates on the Pittsburgh Crawfords, they were considered a mighty powerful duo. Posters for the Crawfords read, JOSH GIBSON AND SATCHEL PAIGE— THE GREATEST BATTERY IN BASEBALL. GIBSON GUARANTEED TO HIT TWO HOME RUNS AND PAIGE GUARANTEED TO STRIKE OUT THE FIRST NINE MEN.

"Someday we'll meet up and see who's best," they would often joke with each other. In 1942, soon after Satchel's return to the road, they got their chance.

It was September 10, 1942, the second game of the Negro World Series. Satch's team, the Kansas City Monarchs, was in a heated best-of-seven matchup against the Homestead Grays, led by Josh Gibson. Toward the end of the game, Satch decided to raise the stakes. With two outs in the inning and one man on base, he walked two players so the bases would be loaded when Josh Gibson came up to bat. "Someday we'll meet up and see who's best" rang in Satch's ears as he prepared to face the man who would now determine the fate of his team and Satch's reputation. Satchel called to Josh, "Remember back when we were playing with the Crawfords and you said you was the best hitter in the world and I was the best pitcher?"

"Yeah, I remember," Josh called back.

"Well, now we're going to see what's what," Satch said.

With a ball in hand and a grin on his face, Satch told Josh, "I'm gonna throw a fastball letter high."

"Strike one!"

Josh shook his head, tightened his grip on the bat, and resumed his position as he tried to stare into Satchel's eyes.

But Satch stared straight ahead at Josh's knees. His coach back at the Mount Meigs School had always told him, "Look at the knees, Satch. Every weakness a batter has, you can spot in the knees."

"Now I'm gonna throw this one a little faster and belt high," Satch said during his windup.

"Strike two!"

In typical Satch style, he called in a mocking voice, "Now I got you oh-and-two and I'm supposed to knock you down, but instead I'm gonna throw a pea at your knee."

"Strike three!"

Josh never moved the bat. Satch slowly exhaled the breath he'd been holding since the windup. It was over. He'd done what he'd come to do.

"Nobody hits Satchel's fastball," he said through a smile as bright as the sun. "And nobody ever will."

Throughout his life, Satch had always felt that most rules were made just to keep him from getting his fair share. Major leaguers who'd seen him play told Satch, "We could use you, if only you were white." The first time he heard it, his stomach boiled over till it made his insides hurt. But, as always, pitching was his medicine for all his aches and pains. When the rules against blacks playing in the major leagues finally changed, Satch was one of the first in line to get what he felt he had earned. On July 7, 1948, his forty-second birthday, the Cleveland Indians offered Satch a gift he'd never forget: a pitching spot in the major leagues.

Satch accepted, but he had made and followed his own rules for so long, it was hard for him to play someone else's game. It seemed like the majors were all about rules. Rules about exercise—"Shaking hands with the catcher is all the exercise I need," Satch would insist. Rules about following the catcher's signals—"There ain't no need for signs. All you gotta do is show me a glove and hold it still, I'll hit it," he would tell his coach. And more rules about being on time for practices, for games.

In exhibition games during the off-seasons, Satch had left no doubt in anyone's mind who was the best pitcher in any league. Other players would watch him, some even studied him. But for Satch good playing had nothing to do with rules. Pitching was a gift he was born with. It was buried deep in his bones, and you couldn't learn it or even shake it; it was just there.

It was only two seasons later when Satch pitched his final innings for the major leagues. His age and his difficulty with the rules made both of those seasons extra challenging, but even with the best of his pitching years behind him, he gave the Cleveland Indians a boost. He pitched for them in a World Series and throughout both seasons. All who wanted a glimpse of the tall, lean legend named Satch could get it for just the price of a ticket. From fans to future players, everyone who saw him play took away images so fresh and clear, they might as well have been color snapshots.

When the cheers started to fade, Satch never did. For the next twelve years he played on any team that would have him and his satchel full of pitches. In 1953, baseball finally closed its doors to Satch. The Baseball Hall of Fame in Cooperstown, New York, opened theirs to him in 1971. He was the first Negro League player they honored and he had one of the longest and brightest careers in baseball history.

# ★ VITAL STATISTICS ★

**FULL NAME:**

*Leroy "Satchel" Paige*

**BIRTHDATE:**

*Believed to be July 7, 1906 (No one is sure of his actual birthdate; Satchel offered conflicting dates.)*

**MOTTO:**

*"Ain't no man can avoid being average, but ain't no man got to be common."*

**FAMILY:**

*Married Lahoma Brown in 1941; had five daughters and one son*

**SPECIAL ACHIEVEMENTS:**

*First player from Negro Leagues to be inducted into Baseball Hall of Fame;
first black to pitch in a major league World Series;
Sporting News magazine's Rookie of the Year*

**OVERALL CONTRIBUTION:**

*Satchel Paige is best remembered for bringing to the game of baseball a unique combination
of showmanship and sportsmanship. He infused the Negro Leagues with an energy
that helped sustain it through the leanest of times.*

**DEATH DATE:**

*June 8, 1982*

# BIBLIOGRAPHY

Holway, John B. *Black Diamonds: Life in the Negro Leagues from the Men Who Lived It.* New York: Stadium Books, 1991.

McKissack, Fredrick, Jr., and Patricia C. McKissack. *Black Diamond: The Story of the Negro Baseball Leagues.* New York: Scholastic, 1994.

Paige, Leroy (Satchel) as told to David Lipman. *Maybe I'll Pitch Forever: A Great Baseball Player Tells the Hilarious Story Behind the Legend.* Lincoln, Nebr.: University of Nebraska Press, 1993.

Peterson, Robert. *Only the Ball Was White: A History of Legendary Black Players and All-Black Professional Teams.* New York: Oxford University Press, 1970.

Ribowsky, Mark. *Don't Look Back: Satchel Paige in the Shadows of Baseball.* New York: Simon & Schuster, 1994.

Ward, Geoffrey C. and Ken Burns. *Baseball: An Illustrated History.* New York: Alfred A. Knopf, 1994.

ALADDIN PAPERBACKS
An imprint of Simon & Schuster Children's Publishing Division
1230 Avenue of the Americas, New York, NY 10020

First Aladdin Paperbacks edition January 2003

Also available in a Simon & Schuster Books for Young Readers hardcover edition.
The Library of Congress has cataloged the hardcover edition as follows:
Ransome, Lesa Cline. Satchel Paige / Lesa Cline-Ransome ; illustrated by James E. Ransome. p. cm. Summary: Examines the life of the legendary baseball player, who was the first African-American to pitch in a Major League World Series.
ISBN 0-689-81151-9 (hc)
1. Paige, Leroy 1906— Juvenile literature. 2. Baseball players—United States—Biography—Juvenile literature. [1. Paige, Leroy, 1906—. 2. Baseball players. 3. Afro-Americans—Biography.] I. Ransome, James E., ill. II. Title. GV856.P3R35    2000
796.357'092—dc21   [B]  97-13790
ISBN 978-0-689-85681-5 (Aladdin pbk.)
0911 SCP